# My Spooky Halloween

## Activity and Sticker Book

BLOOMSBURY
Activity Books
NEW YORK   LONDON   NEW DELHI   SYDNEY

Can you figure out which
spider can get to the fly
through the maze?

# Only one shadow matches the witch. Can you find it?

4

to the witch's washing line.

Use stickers to give the pumpkins faces. Draw a few scary ones, too!

# Match the shadows to the shapes.

Can you find 4 owls, 5 broomsticks,

and 1 cauldron in this picture?

Using the code on this page, write a spooky message on the opposite page.

Draw silly shoes, boots, and
hats on the spooky witches.

Spot the differences
between the two castles.

There are 8 to find.

Using the grid as a guide, copy and color
the spooky mummy onto the opposite page.

16

Use stickers to fill the witches' cauldron with yucky things to make a potion.

Spot the one that is
different in each group.

Complete the picture by adding
the spooky owl stickers.

22

Use stickers to add spooky people and creatures to the party.

24

Draw or find stickers of horns and tails to add to the cats and dogs.

Count the cats, bats, and spiders and add more spooky stickers to the page.

Follow the lines to see which present each spooky owl is taking to the party.

Draw a haunted house in the middle of the spooky forest.

Use stickers to design and decorate
a wanted poster for something spooky.
It could be a witch, a skeleton, a mummy,
or a made-up monster.

32

Pages 26-27

Pages 24-25

Page 32